# No Home for Shannon

WRITTEN BY

## MARILYN D.
ANDERSON

*To the memory of*
*Tama O'Tyshe*

**Publishing Group ™**

Fifth printing by Willowisp Press 1997.

Published by PAGES Publishing Group
801 94th Avenue North, St. Petersburg, Florida 33702

Printed in the United States of America

Willowisp Press®

6 8 10 9 7 5

ISBN 0-87406-842-8

# Chapter
# ONE

Holly Church felt as if she had been waiting in the outfield forever. She hated softball, but her Phys. Ed. class seemed to play it every day. The game was especially boring today because her friend, Terri, was on the other team.

Suddenly, Holly heard a mighty "crack" and something went whizzing over her head. It sailed over the bushes at the end of the playground, landing in the pasture beyond.

Immediately, Holly's team started to yell at her. "Hey, Holly, wake up! Don't just stand there. Get the ball."

Holly turned and crashed blindly through the bushes. She was thinking so hard about the ball

that she almost ran into something. It was big, tan, and furry. Before she screamed, she realized it was just a dog.

The pale gold dog had the missing softball in his mouth. His long coat was a mass of cockle-burs. His wide, intelligent face was full of expression. It seemed to say, "Are you friendly? I need your help."

Then Holly heard someone coming. The dog heard it, too. He dropped the ball and ran behind some bushes.

A moment later Mike Brown was standing beside Holly. He saw the ball at once and scooped it up in his glove. "Girls," he groaned as he turned to go back to the game.

Holly waited to see if the dog would return. She was curious about him. What was he doing here anyway?

For a long time now Holly had wanted a dog of her own. Every Christmas and every birthday she had asked for a puppy. It seemed her parents always had some excuse. But, wondered Holly, what if I found my own dog?

"What's up?" came a voice from beyond the bushes. It sounded like snoopy Amy Baker.

"Uh, nothing," Holly answered quickly. "I was just looking around."

"Oh, yeah?" the voice said. "You'd better get back to the game. Miss Walker is getting upset."

"All right," Holly sighed. "I'm coming." She turned for a last look and there was the dog.

His tail was wagging uncertainly and he was not very far away. Holly wanted to pet him, but she did have to get back. She hesitated.

"Miss Walker says to come now," the voice insisted.

"All right," Holly answered angrily. Then she said to the dog, "Stay here. I'll be back soon."

Holly told Terri about the dog as soon as she had a chance. "Come with me after school," she whispered. "I've got to see if he's still there."

"But I've got a piano lesson," Terri protested. "And what's so interesting about a stray dog?"

"Wait until you see him," Holly told her. "He's

beautiful! I think he's a golden retriever and he seems to be lost."

"So?" Terri answered.

"So he might be hungry. He might need our help," said Holly.

"All right," Terri agreed. "I'll take a quick look with you. I just hope he doesn't bite us."

Later the girls slipped through the bushes and into the pasture. At first they saw nothing unusual.

"Here, dog," Holly called softly.

That made Terri laugh. "He's not going to come. You don't even know his name," she giggled.

"Shhh," Holly insisted. "You'll scare him for sure."

They waited a few more minutes before Terri nudged Holly. "Look over there," she hissed.

Holly turned to see the dog almost behind her. Its tail wagged slowly.

"Good dog," Holly said softly. "I saved you part of my lunch. Do you like bologna sandwiches?" She threw him a piece.

The dog cocked his head to one side. He stared at Holly for a minute. He looked at the food and licked his chops.

"It's okay. You can have it," Holly told him.

The dog then walked over and gulped down the sandwich. His eyes pleaded for more. Holly threw him another piece and another. Soon the dog walked right up to them.

"His coat is a mess," Terri breathed.

"I'll say," Holly nodded. "I wonder where he got all those burrs."

"He's wearing a collar but no tags," Terri noticed. "Maybe some hunter lost him."

"I'll bet you're right," Holly agreed. "Let's take him home."

"Your folks would love that," Terri snorted. "Besides, I've got to get to my piano lesson. Bye."

"Terri!" Holly begged. "You've got to help me."

"Bye," called Terri, and she disappeared through the bushes.

The dog was sitting now and he was watching Holly intently. His eyes looked so sad that she just knew he was hungry.

"If you come to my house, I'll find you some more food," she promised. The dog continued to sit and stare. He seemed to be thinking hard.

"Come on," Holly called as she started toward home.

When she reached the playground, the big yellow dog was at her side. His mouth was opened in a wide grin and he trotted eagerly.

# Chapter

## TWO

When Holly got home she took the dog right to the refrigerator. There were a lot of leftovers from yesterday's dinner. Her mother always made more food than they could eat. Holly knew her mom wouldn't be home right away. So she made up a plate of food for the dog.

When the dog finished eating, Holly gave him some water. Then she took him outside. "Maybe no one will ever come for you," she told him. "Maybe you can stay with me always. I'd better clean you up so Mom will like you."

Holly found an old comb and brush to use on the burrs. The dog whined when she pulled on his hair. He licked her hand when she stopped. Soon Holly had a big pile of burrs and the dog looked much better.

"You really are a handsome fellow," she said proudly.

The dog poked his nose under her hand. She laughed and said, "Want to be petted now, eh? That's what I call a hint."

She stroked his head and played with his long, silky ears. She patted his sturdy sides. The dog wiggled with happiness.

Soon a car pulled into the driveway. Holly knew it was her mom because her dad was on another trip for the Navy.

"Look what I found," said Holly the minute her mother appeared.

Mrs. Church stared and demanded, "Where did he come from?"

Holly shrugged. "He followed me home. Isn't he pretty?"

Her mother made a face. "I guess he's all right as dogs go," she said. "But we don't need

a dog. You'd better get rid of him."

"But, Mom," Holly sputtered. "I can't just throw him out in the street. He might get hurt."

"Then I'll call the animal shelter," her mom answered quickly.

"Oh, they must be closed by now," Holly said desperately. "Couldn't he stay here until tomorrow?"

Her mother started to say "no," but she saw the pleading in Holly's eyes. Instead she sighed and said, "All right. I guess he can stay in the garage tonight. But tomorrow we'll try to find his owner."

"And if we can't find his owner . . .," Holly began.

"No, you may not keep him," her mother finished.

"Oh, Mom, please?" Holly begged.

"I don't want to talk about it," Mrs. Church told her. "I'm tired and hungry. Just get him out of my way."

Holly nodded. "I will. I will and thanks."

Her mom was going into the house when Holly quickly said, "Gee, I'd better get him some dog food. Can I go to the store?"

"I suppose," Mrs. Church said. "You'll have to use your own money, though." And she disappeared into the house.

Holly dashed in after her to get the money. She was out again in minutes. The dog pranced around so eagerly that she knew he wanted to go along.

It would be fun to take him, Holly thought, but I'll need a leash. She didn't want him to run out into the street. All she really needed was something to slip through the dog's collar. Then she thought of her belt. "That would work," she muttered. She pulled the belt out of her jeans and reached for the dog.

Suddenly, he was gone. She looked around and found him hiding under her mom's car. She knelt down and tried to talk him out.

"What's the matter?" she coaxed. "Don't you want to come along? Did something scare you?"

Then Holly remembered the belt. She was

still carrying it. Could that be it? She put the belt back in her jeans and knelt down again.

"I'm sorry. See, no more belt," she told him. "Come on out."

Finally the dog wiggled out and licked her hand. Holly decided to put him in the garage. She went to the store alone.

On the way she wondered about the dog and the belt. Maybe he wasn't lost at all. Maybe he ran away on purpose.

When Holly told her mother about it, she didn't pay much attention.

"Do you think someone hit him with a belt?" Holly wondered.

"I doubt it," her mom said. "Why would anyone do that?"

Holly had no answer.

The next morning was Saturday. Holly wanted to spend as much time with the dog as possible. She thought he would probably be gone by noon. She went out to the garage early. The dog greeted her with a happy wiggle. Then he made strange noises that sounded as if he were trying to sing for her.

The dog was so excited when Holly let him out of the garage that he bounded around the yard in huge circles. When he brought her a stick, she threw it for him. The dog's ears flew out behind him as he charged after it. Each time Holly threw a stick the dog's body trembled with eagerness. Each time he brought the stick quickly to her and begged to go again. When her mom finally called her for breakfast, Holly and the dog were resting in a cozy heap.

"Sorry to spoil the fun," Mrs. Church smiled. "You two do make a cute pair."

Holly put the dog in the garage again and went into the house to wash up. Her mom seemed to be in a better mood this morning. Maybe she'll change her mind about keeping the dog, Holly thought hopefully.

Between sips of coffee, her mother announced, "I'll call the animal shelter right after we eat. The longer that dog stays here the harder it will be for you to give him up."

Holly pushed her eggs around on her plate. "What if they don't want him?" she asked.

"They'll take him," Mrs. Church said firmly.

"But why can't I have a dog?" Holly demanded.

"Let's not start that again," her mother told her. "Dogs are a lot of trouble."

"I would feed him and take him for his walks," Holly insisted.

"There are other problems with having a dog," her mother explained. "They make messes on the lawn. They dig holes. They make traveling a problem."

"I still want a dog . . .," Holly said stubbornly.

"I'll call the shelter right now," her mom interrupted.

The man at the shelter checked his list of missing dogs. "I don't see any male golden retrievers on it," he told Mrs. Church. "Still, that doesn't mean his owner isn't looking for him. Lots of dogs are lost during hunting season. It takes us a while to catch up."

17

"I see," said Holly's mom. "Well, when can you come and get him?"

The man was silent for a minute. "I guess I could come this afternoon," he admitted. "It's just that we are so crowded right now. I'd have to put your dog in a very small pen with three other dogs. Is there any chance you could keep him for a few more days?"

Mrs. Church frowned. "A few more days? What are we going to do with him?" she asked.

"It would be just until some of these dogs are gone," he assured her. "You could place an ad in the newspaper and see if anyone claims him," the man suggested.

Mrs. Church hesitated, then she sighed. "All right," she agreed. "We'll keep him for a while longer, but let us know as soon as you have more room."

"Yea!" Holly cheered as her mom hung up the telephone.

"It's just for a few days," Mrs. Church reminded her. "Remember that."

# Chapter
# THREE

Holly told Terri the good news. "So I get to keep him a little longer," she finished.

"That's great," Terri said, smiling. "He really is a nice dog."

Holly nodded. "And I feel sorry for him, too." Then she told Terri about the dog and the belt.

"Gosh," Terri breathed. "That sounds bad."

"Doesn't it?" said Holly. "If his owner beats him, I hope the guy never comes."

"But there isn't much you can do about it," Terri pointed out. "Besides, your mom doesn't want a dog, right?"

"Mom says 'no' so far," Holly admitted.

"Then he'd have to go to the animal shelter

eventually," Terri said.

"Yeah, I guess so," Holly agreed.

"Then you'd better hope his owner does come," Terri said seriously.

Holly looked puzzled. "Why do you say that? What's the matter with the animal shelter?"

"Don't you know what they do to dogs there?" Terri insisted.

Holly thought a minute. "Well, sure, they take care of them."

Terri snorted. "Of course, they take care of them . . . for a while. Then the dogs that aren't claimed are put to sleep."

"They are?" gasped Holly. "That's terrible. How can they do such a thing?"

"Well, no one can afford to feed every stray dog," Terri explained. "The shelter has to make room for the next batch."

"Yuk," said Holly loudly. "That puts this poor dog in a terrible spot."

"Right," Terri nodded.

"If his owner doesn't come, my folks have to

take him," Holly said desperately.

The girls played with the dog for a while and then decided to take him to the park. "But I still don't have a leash," Holly remembered.

"Your neighbor, Mr. Fields, has a dog. Maybe he has one," Terri suggested.

Mr. Fields looked surprised when Holly asked to borrow a leash. "I didn't know you had a dog," he said.

"I don't," Holly said. "I found one yesterday."

"It's a hunting dog," Terri added.

Suddenly, Mr. Fields looked interested. "Oh, a hunting dog? I'd like to see it," he said eagerly.

The girls agreed and the man followed them to Holly's garage.

"He's a beauty," Mr. Fields said. "Someone must be looking for him."

"Do you know much about hunting dogs?" Terri asked.

"Well, not exactly," the man shrugged. "However, I've been to a few field trials. That's where dogs compete in retrieving birds."

"How did the owners treat their dogs?" Holly asked suddenly.

Mr. Fields gave her an odd look. "Why do you ask? Hunters take good care of their dogs."

"Oh, I was just wondering, that's all," she mumbled. "I noticed this dog is afraid of belts, and I thought maybe . . ."

"Hmmmm," said Mr. Fields. "I have to admit that some hunters get a little rough with their dogs."

"With a belt?" Holly demanded.

"Sometimes," her neighbor admitted. "They do have to discipline the dogs. However, most hunters know that golden retrievers are very sensitive. A beating might ruin their spirit."

"I see," said Holly. She didn't want to hear anymore. "Thanks for the leash. I guess we'd better be going."

"Glad to help," Mr. Fields nodded. "Say, are you going to keep this dog if the owner doesn't show up?"

"I want to," Holly said sadly. "So far it doesn't

look like my folks will let me. Maybe you'd like him."

Mr. Fields shook his head. "Sorry. I'd like to, but I already have my cocker spaniel. Silky wouldn't take kindly to another dog in the house and neither would Mrs. Fields."

"Too bad," said Holly.

"Yeah, too bad," Terri agreed.

The dog trotted happily on the leash all the way to the park. But the girls were quiet for a long time.

Finally, Terri said, "You know, it seems weird to keep calling him 'dog.' Couldn't we give him a name?"

"Yeah, let's make up a name," Holly said eagerly. "How about calling him Shannon?"

"Shannon?" Terri protested. "That's a girl's name."

"It is not," Holly insisted. "I once knew a boy named Shannon and I really liked the name."

Terri shrugged. "Well, why not? It won't be his real name anyway. Shannon it is."

"Come on, Shannon," Holly said lightly. "This is the park and we're going to have fun."

There were tons of people in the park. Old people, mothers with babies, and kids of all ages were enjoying one of the last warm days of the year. The girls looked for a spot to put their blanket.

Suddenly a Frisbee sailed by and Shannon became a blur of gold. He yanked the leash out of Holly's hand as he grabbed the toy.

"That's some dog you've got there," panted a teenage boy. He smiled as he took the Frisbee from Shannon. Then he said to the girls, "Maybe you and your dog would like to play with us."

Holly and Terri looked at each other. Both girls nodded their heads eagerly and followed the boy. At first Holly and Shannon were a team. Holly threw the Frisbee and Shannon caught it when it was their turn. But it was so much fun to watch Shannon catch the Frisbee that soon everyone threw it only to him. He could catch any kind of a toss and he did it with great joy.

When the girls left the park it was late. "I've never had such a good time," Holly said happily.

"I'll say," Terri agreed. "Those older kids would never have asked us to play if it hadn't been for Shannon."

"Oh, I wish I could keep him," Holly groaned. "He was just born to belong to someone like me."

"I agree with that," Terri said. "It's your folks you've got to convince."

# Chapter
# FOUR

The next few days passed quickly. Holly's mom seemed to accept Shannon, and now her dad was due home. Holly wanted him to like the dog, too, so she brushed Shannon's golden hair with extra care that evening. Then she waited nervously for her father to arrive.

"Dad's here," Holly called at last. Mrs. Church smiled and laid down her crossword puzzle to follow Holly. Her dad had a little present and a hug for each of them. Her mom had several important things to tell him.

Then Holly's dad looked at her and said with a grin, "And what have you been up to?"

"There's something new around here. Want

to see it?" she answered hopefully.

"I suppose so," he agreed. "Where is it?"

"In the garage," she told him. "Come on."

Holly led the way and opened the door slowly. Suddenly, Shannon shot out. He almost knocked Mr. Church down in his excitement. He wagged his tail and jumped around joyfully.

"Get that dog away from me," her dad yelped. "What kind of a surprise is this?"

"Now, Jim . . .," her mom began.

"Betty, you know I don't like dogs," Holly's dad snapped angrily.

"Shannon is really a nice dog," Holly begged. "Please give him a chance."

But her dad headed for the house. "Your mother and I have something to discuss," he said to Holly. "You stay here."

Holly was crushed. She hadn't expected her father to get so upset. Now her parents would argue. Shannon would have to go. *What a mess,* Holly said to herself.

It seemed like hours before Mrs. Church

told Holly to come in. Her dad was sitting in his favorite chair with a newspaper in front of his face. He did not look up.

Her mom sat down on the sofa. She looked over at her husband, who continued to read. She said to Holly, "I've been telling your father about you and Shannon. He really doesn't like dogs, but we do want to be fair to you. We have decided that Shannon can stay here if his owner doesn't come to claim him."

Holly started to say, "Thank you—"

"Just remember," her father interrupted. "He's not to come in the house or get in my way if he stays."

"Oh, I'll keep him out of trouble," Holly promised. "You'll see."

Mr. Church was home for the next few days and he did try to be fair. He even rigged up a wire between two trees for Shannon. Holly could tie the dog's leash to the wire and it would slide back and forth as he ran.

Although Mr. Church tried to ignore the dog,

Shannon kept trying to make friends. Whenever he saw Holly's dad, the dog wagged his tail and seemed to smile. The day her father had to leave again, Holly saw him stare at the dog for a long time. Then he walked away without saying a word.

Each day Holly's hopes of keeping Shannon grew. His owner still hadn't come and it had been over a week.

Friday was an extra-pretty autumn day. Holly took the dog for a long walk. It was almost dark when they turned the last corner toward home. The closer they got to the house, the more Shannon began to hold back. He began to whine.

Holly couldn't figure out what was wrong until she saw a strange car in the driveway. The big, expensive car seemed to tell her that something bad was about to happen.

Before she reached the living room, Holly heard a man's voice say, "I've been looking for that dog for over two weeks. If he weren't so darn valuable, I wouldn't have bothered. I can't believe he came this far."

The girl looked into the living room and saw a big man about fifty years old. His clothes were soft and expensive, but his eyes were hard.

Her mom saw Holly and said nervously, "Oh, here she is now. This is my daughter. Holly, this is Mr. Wendell Burns."

Mr. Burns looked down at the girl and said, "I understand you found a golden retriever."

"Yes," she almost whispered.

"Where did you find him?" the man asked.

"He came to our school yard," Holly explained.

The man groaned. "I suppose he wanted to play and everybody had him retrieving junk."

Holly was surprised. "Well, not exactly," she stammered. "But your dog does like to play."

"Worst thing in the world for a hunting dog," Mr. Burns complained. "It gets them all mixed up. You ask them to bring in a bird and they bring you a stick instead."

"Does your dog like to hunt?" Holly asked.

Mr. Burns gave a little jerk. "What?" he asked crossly. "How do I know if he likes to hunt? I do know he's given me nothing but trouble lately. Where is he anyway?"

"We don't know if it is your dog, yet," Mrs. Church said quietly.

"No, we don't," the man admitted. "Let's find out right now. Let me see him, please."

As Holly led the way, she prayed that Shannon wasn't the right dog. She didn't want to give him to Mr. Burns.

At first they didn't see the dog in the garage because Shannon was hiding under the car again. Holly had to drag him out. She felt awful about it, too.

Mr. Burns took one look at the dog and said, "That's my dog. I have papers in the car to prove it if you want to see them."

"No, that won't be necessary," Mrs. Church told him. "We can see that he knows you."

It made Holly sick to see Shannon looking so miserable. She tried not to cry as she said fiercely, "I hope you treat him nicely."

"I don't believe in babying a dog," the man

33

snapped back. Then he roughly examined his property. "The dog does seem to be in good shape," Mr. Burns said as he straightened up. "Here's twenty dollars for your trouble."

With that, the man pushed some money at Holly and dragged Shannon to his car. Holly took the money like a robot and fought back her tears.

As the car pulled away, her mom said grimly, "I feel like crying, too. That man doesn't deserve to have a dog."

When the car was out of sight, Holly remembered the money in her hand. It felt dirty to her. "Here, Mom," she said. "I don't want this. I want Shannon." Then she burst into big sobs and ran into the house.

The house seemed much too quiet from then on. Holly just moped around all week. Even her mom seemed to miss Shannon.

When Mr. Church came home, he didn't say much about it at first. Finally he remarked, "I'd rather have the dog than all this gloom."

Holly looked up from a boring TV show. "It's

not the same around here without Shannon," she said bitterly.

"Maybe not," her dad agreed. "But we couldn't keep him. He did belong to Mr. Burns, you know."

"I suppose so," Holly sniffed. "I bet you're glad about it, too. Go on, admit it. You're glad Shannon is gone."

Her dad thought for a minute. Then he said, "You're right. I wasn't comfortable with a dog around."

"That's what I thought. How can you be so mean?" Holly sobbed suddenly. Then she began to really cry and ran from the room.

"What did I say to cause that?" her father asked.

# Chapter
# FIVE

Shannon had been gone for several months and the worst part of the winter was over. On the way to school one day, Terri pulled out a newspaper clipping. "Hey, do you want to go to this?" she asked.

Holly took the paper and read: "Center City Dog Show Saturday. Over 900 entries." The story went on to tell where the show would be held and some of the classes that would be included.

"Well, do you want to go?" Terri asked again.

Holly shrugged. "I don't know," she said sadly. "I don't like to think about dogs since Shannon left."

"Aw, come on," Terri coaxed. "My mom said

she would drive us. We can eat lunch out."

Holly thought for a few more minutes. "Well, okay," she mumbled. "I guess I can't avoid dogs for the rest of my life."

Terri smiled. "That's the spirit. It will be fun. You'll see."

*  *  *  *  *  *

The dog show was held at the huge Center City Arena. It was a noisy sea of confusion as the girls checked their programs.

"Let's watch the obedience ring," Terri suggested.

"All right," Holly agreed. "I like to see dogs do interesting things."

The girls located the ring for Utility Dogs. The most highly trained animals at the whole show would be in that class.

Poodles, shelties, and dobermans performed. But the best dog was a golden retriever named Gentle George. The dog was more reddish than

Shannon had been, but his bounce was the same. He seemed so happy to please his mistress that sometimes he jumped into the air as he obeyed her commands. He sailed over jumps, retrieved a dumbbell, and picked out the glove with his owner's scent. He never made a mistake. The girls clapped long and hard when George won his class.

"I'll bet Shannon would be good at that," Holly said.

"Mr. Burns wouldn't have the patience to train him," Terri reminded her.

The girls decided to check the program again. Terri noticed that golden retrievers were being shown in Ring 2, but Holly didn't want to see them. Terri started to read out loud the names of dogs and owners. Some were really funny.

Suddenly Holly said, "Wait a minute. Did you say Wendell Burns has a dog here? Is it a golden retriever?"

Terri checked the program. "Why, yes, the dog's name is Bald Mountain Golden Boy," she read.

"My gosh," gasped Holly. "That could be Shannon. Come on."

The girls hurried up to Ring 2 just as the dogs were entering. Holly looked all around for Mr. Burns, but she didn't see him.

"False alarm," she panted to Terri. Then she noticed a pale gold dog at the far end of the ring. It was looking at her, too. "That looks like Shannon," she whispered to Terri. "Do you suppose Mr. Burns sold him?"

The beautiful dog Holly was looking at began to get excited. His tail wagged wildly and he craned his neck to watch her. He paid no attention to the man at the end of his leash.

Then each dog was asked to trot halfway around the judging area and back to the judge. There they were to pose for inspection. Each dog put on a fine show.

Shannon started out well because he was headed toward Holly. He was eager to get to her so he trotted boldly. But as the handler turned, the dog began to lag behind. When the judge tried to get his attention, Shannon kept wiggling and stretching to see Holly. At last the judge gave up and gave Shannon last place.

As the dogs left the ring, the girls followed and tried to get closer to them. They could hear Shannon's handler mumbling, "I'll teach you to ignore me, you mutt. Burns said you were nothing but trouble."

"What should we do?" Terri whispered. "That man sounds mean."

"Come on," Holly hissed back. "We've got to catch them before he does anything to Shannon."

They followed the man to the parking lot and saw him tie Shannon to the side of the dog trailer. He was just taking out a long strap when Holly yelled, "Stop!"

The man looked up and demanded angrily, "Who says? Are you the brats this dumb mutt wanted to gawk at? You kids ruined that class for me. Maybe I ought to give you a whipping, too."

"We didn't mean any harm and you have no

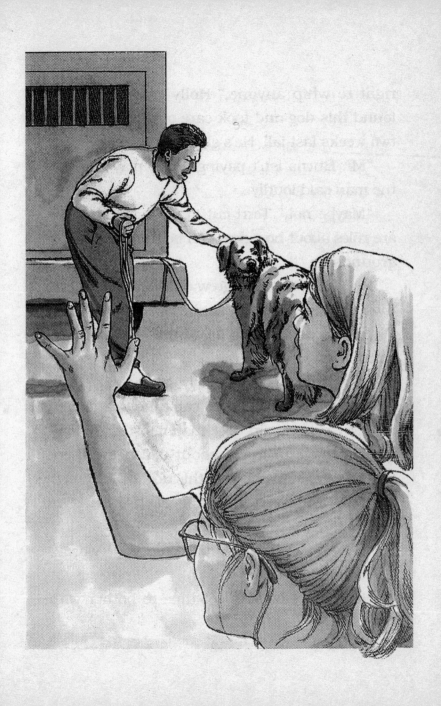

right to whip anyone," Holly said angrily. "I found this dog and took care of him for almost two weeks last fall. He's glad to see me."

"Mr. Burns isn't paying me to play games," the man said loudly.

"Maybe not," Terri cut in, "but I'll bet there are rules about how dogs can be treated on show grounds."

Suddenly the man grew quiet. He eyed Terri thoughtfully. Then he said, "I'll tell you what. I'll go easy on this dog if you two will make me a promise."

"Oh sure, anything," Holly said eagerly.

"You girls must never come near a golden retriever class again," the man insisted. "I don't want to have to worry about you being there the next time I'm showing this dog."

Holly and Terri looked at each other. "We promise," they said together.

"How do we know you'll keep your word?" Terri added.

"Humph, I haven't got time to bother with

this dog," the man grunted. "I've got a lot of dogs to show today. You're wasting my time."

The man stuffed Shannon into a cage. He pulled out a cute beagle from the next one. "Right now I've got to get this dog ready, so beat it," he snarled.

"You bet," said Terri as she gave Holly a push.

The girls walked away until they were out of sight. Then, they watched the man from behind some cars. When he left with the beagle, Holly wanted to go to Shannon.

"Don't do it," Terri told her. "You can't help him now. It will only get his hopes up."

"I guess you're right," Holly sniffed. "I wish I had never come to this show. Then I wouldn't know how miserable he is."

43

# Chapter
# SIX

Several weeks later Holly was coming home to a dark house. It was a windy March day and she was eager to get into the warmth of the house. As she ran up the steps, a big furry mass suddenly landed on her. It licked her face and nearly knocked her down.

"Shannon," she gasped. "How did you get here?"

The dog sat before her and began to make his singing noises. It almost sounded as if he was trying to tell Holly something.

She dropped down and gave the dog a big hug. "I don't care how you got here," Holly said happily. "I'm so glad to see you."

Then she began to think. She knew Mr. Burns would soon come looking for his property. Her mom would insist Shannon go back if she found him here. Holly decided to hide the dog and not tell anyone. Then she thought of the perfect place. She would just have time to take Shannon there before her mom got home.

Holly gave Terri a call and said, "Meet me in the old barn behind your house right away. I've got to talk to you."

"In the barn? What are you up to?" Terri asked. "Holly? Holly—"

But Holly had hung up. She gathered up some canned dog food left from last fall and several old pans. She took a jar of water and put a rope on Shannon.

"All right," she told him. "We've got to go now. This may be your only chance."

"Oh, my gosh," Terri gasped when she saw Shannon. "I might have guessed. What are you planning?"

"You know I can't give him back," Holly said

grimly. "I thought he could stay in this barn for a while. Then I could truthfully say I don't have him."

"You could get in a lot of trouble," Terri warned. "Mr. Burns could say you stole the dog if he finds out."

"I don't care," Holly insisted. "He's not going back to people who mistreat him."

Terri sighed. "All right. What do you want me to do?"

"Nothing really," Holly told her. "Just make sure your parents don't come back here."

"That won't be hard," Terri assured her. "There's nothing in this barn except hay."

"Good," said Holly. "I'll try to think of another place soon."

"Then let's get him fed and get home before someone misses us," Terri urged.

"Right," Holly nodded. "Mr. Burns might come calling anytime now."

Holly had just started her homework when Mr. Burns's car pulled in the driveway. Her mother was surprised to see him. "Won't you come in?" Holly heard her say.

"Is my dog here?" the man demanded.

"Your dog?" Mrs. Church said coolly. "No, I haven't seen your dog."

"Well, he's missing again," Mr. Burns stormed. "He got away from the handler who was showing him."

"That's too bad," Holly's mom said evenly.

"Is your little girl home?" Mr. Burns wanted to know. "Maybe she knows something about all this."

"I think she'd have said something," her mom said doubtfully. "Holly, will you come here please?"

Holly came out slowly. She didn't want to lie, but she wouldn't send Shannon back.

"Mr. Burns wants to know if we have his dog," said Mrs. Church. "I told him I haven't seen it."

Holly looked the man straight in the eye and said, "Your dog isn't here."

"There, you see?" said her mom.

"All right. I'm sorry to have bothered you," said Mr. Burns. As he turned to go, he added, "Please call me if he does come."

The next morning Holly crept out of the house very early. She made it to the barn without anyone seeing her and fed Shannon.

"Maybe we can go for a walk tonight after dark," she told him. "I can't risk having you seen."

That day it seemed every teacher assigned a ton of homework. There would be no time to exercise Shannon tonight.

By the next morning, the dog was wild to get out. He tried to sneak out as soon as Holly opened the door.

"Tonight for sure," she promised him.

But it rained all day and night. By morning everything was wet and Holly was running late.

*Today's Friday. I'll have time to walk Shannon tonight for sure,* she thought.

Holly's father was there when she got home from school. He wanted to take the family out to dinner. They would go to a show afterward. Her mom was excited about going, but Holly was worried about Shannon.

She said, "Um, I need to take something over to Terri's house first. Could you wait for me?"

"No problem. We'll drive by Terri's house and you can drop it off," her dad suggested.

Holly knew she'd have to think of something else fast. She sat in the backseat of the car on the way over. She was writing a note to Terri to put inside the book that she'd brought. The note asked Terri to feed Shannon and take him for a walk if possible. But Terri's house was dark when they got there. No one was home.

"I have sort of a stomach ache," Holly said vaguely. "Maybe you should go without me."

"A stomach ache?" her mom asked suspiciously. "Why didn't you say something about it earlier?"

"Umm," Holly hesitated. "I ah . . ." But she couldn't keep lying. "I guess I'd better tell you the truth," she said miserably. "Shannon came back.

I hid him in Terri's old barn. I have to give him some food before I can go to a movie. He needs exercise, too."

"Did you lie to your mother and Mr. Burns?" her dad asked impatiently.

"Well, not exactly," Holly mumbled. "I just said, 'Your dog isn't here.' And he wasn't."

"That's just as bad as lying," her mom insisted. "Why did you do such a thing?"

"I just couldn't send Shannon back," Holly sniffed. "That trainer he's with is awful. I'm sure he ran away because he's miserable."

"Do you think he's happier shut up in a barn?" her dad asked. "You'd better get the dog out of there right now. Then we'll call Mr. Burns with the news that you suddenly found his property."

"Why don't you walk Shannon back to our house?" her mom suggested. "It's not very far and I'm sure he does need the exercise."

"Yeah," Holly said miserably. "Poor Shannon. I've really let him down again."

# Chapter
# SEVEN

M r. and Mrs. Church were in the kitchen drinking coffee when Holly came in. "Everything okay?" her dad asked.

"Just great," Holly mumbled sadly.

"Then come over here," he said. "I have something I want to tell you before we call Mr. Burns."

"I don't think I want to hear it," Holly said dully.

"Well, you're going to hear it," her dad insisted. "I want to explain to you how I feel about dogs."

"It doesn't matter," Holly groaned.

"Please listen," he said. And this time it

sounded more like he was begging than demanding. Holly looked up and waited to see what he would say next.

Her dad began very quietly. "When I was a small boy, I had a long walk home from school every afternoon. There was one dog that barked at me every time, but I never paid much attention. He was always tied up. One day the dog wasn't tied up and he jumped out and attacked me. I might have been killed if someone driving by hadn't stopped to help me. It took an awful lot of stitches to close all of the bites I had. Since that day I've been afraid of dogs."

Holly's eyes grew big. "No wonder you didn't want me to have Shannon," she realized. "You weren't just being mean. Why didn't you tell me before?"

"It's hard for a father to tell his little girl that he's a coward," her dad admitted.

"But I don't think you're a coward," said Holly. "Now I know that you're just like me. I'm afraid of lots of things."

"Thank you, Holly," her dad smiled. "Thank you for understanding."

"Your father and I have been talking again," Holly's mom said cheerfully. "He knows how much Shannon means to you. We've decided to try to buy the dog from Mr. Burns."

Holly could hardly believe her ears. Her dad had just told her that he was afraid of dogs. Suddenly, she knew that both of her parents loved her very much.

"I have about fifty dollars in my savings account. You can use that," she said eagerly.

"A dog like Shannon might be pretty expensive," her dad nodded.

They tried to call Mr. Burns the next morning. A recording told them he was out of town, so Holly's dad left a message.

The next morning was Saturday and the sun was out. It felt so much like spring that the Church family decided to go on a picnic. Mr. Church finally agreed that Shannon could go, too. Before the day was over he actually petted the dog. Shannon just closed his eyes and sat very still while Mr. Church touched him.

Mr. Burns came on Sunday evening. "So he finally got here," the big man said crossly. "I'll see that he doesn't bother you again."

"This dog seems to be a lot of trouble for you," Holly's dad began.

"That's true," Mr. Burns agreed. "I paid a fortune for him because his parents are both champions."

"Holly says you've tried showing him," her dad said. "Any success so far?"

"No, he's acted like a fool at every show," the man complained. "I had planned to make money on his puppies someday. So far I couldn't *give* this dog's puppies away."

"Well, my daughter is quite attached to him," Mr. Church continued. "Would you consider selling the dog?"

Mr. Burns eyes sparkled with interest. "I might be," he said coolly. "Are you prepared to make me an offer?"

Holly's dad hesitated. "I don't know much about what dogs are worth," he admitted.

"I see," Mr. Burns nodded. "Then let me inform you that a dog like this one is worth about five hundred dollars."

Mr. Church looked shocked. "I had no idea a dog could cost so much," he sputtered.

"You can buy registered dogs for one hundred to one hundred and fifty dollars," Mr. Burns explained. "Those are called 'pet-quality.' Show-quality dogs cost more."

"What would you take for Shannon?" Holly's dad asked.

The dog's owner thought for a minute. "In the first place, the dog's name is not Shannon. It's Bald Mountain Golden Boy. He's a son of Bald Mountain Golden Idol. The very least I could take for him would be four hundred dollars."

Mr. Church shook his head. "I can't afford that kind of money for a dog," he said firmly.

"Then you don't want this dog very badly," Mr. Burns laughed.

"What will you do with him?" Mrs. Church demanded.

"I'm putting him with a different trainer," the big man told her. "That last fellow promised a lot, but he couldn't win."

"If Shannon was happy, he'd win," Holly said suddenly.

Mr. Burns snorted. "Dog showing is a game for professionals," he said knowingly. "The dog's business is to win. Nobody asks the dog how he feels about it."

"But the winners always look happy," Holly insisted.

"That's a trick, too," Mr. Burns laughed. "I think I'm wasting my time here."

"Would you take two hundred dollars?" her dad offered.

"No, I wouldn't," the big man said loudly. "Golden Boy cost me more than that as a puppy. Just wait. I'll make money off him yet."

A few minutes later Shannon had been dragged to the car again. He pressed his nose desperately against the car window.

The whole Church family stood and watched the car until it was out of sight. This time they were all sad.

# Chapter
# EIGHT

"Holly! Holly Church, did you hear what I said?"

Holly looked up blankly at Mr. Franklin. She hadn't heard a thing since the beginning of social studies class.

Mr. Franklin shook his head. "I can't understand what's come over you lately," he said. "I hope you can pull yourself together before final tests next week. Otherwise . . ."

"Yes, sir," stammered Holly. "I'll try." She was embarrassed to be singled out in class.

On the way home she told Terri, "I just haven't been able to pay attention to anything since Shannon left. Now I have no idea what's going on in school."

"Let's study together this week," Terri suggested. "I'm sure I can help you. I know how much you miss that dog, but it won't help to flunk."

"Gee, thanks," Holly answered. "Maybe I can still shape up if I try hard enough."

And Holly did try. She and Terri worked hard every night that week. They even studied during the weekend. Terri had paid attention in class and she was a big help.

When finals were over, Holly had passed every test in good shape. Now school was out and it was time to have fun. Instead, Holly had more time to miss Shannon. She didn't feel like doing anything.

One night the phone rang. Her mom answered it. "Hello . . . Yes, I remember your dog . . . Yes, we are still interested in buying him . . ."

Holly sat up fast. Her heart skipped a beat. That could be Mr. Burns. Was there still a chance she could have Shannon?

"No, I'm sorry," her mom said firmly. "Three

hundred dollars is still too much."

Holly slumped back down on the couch.

Then she heard her mom say, "Tomorrow? Well, yes, I guess we could . . . All right, we'll see you there."

Holly jumped up and ran to her mother. "What do you mean?" she squealed. "Where will we see him tomorrow?"

Mrs. Church shook her head and looked puzzled. "That was a very strange call," she told Holly. "Mr. Burns wants us to meet him at Sunnyside Kennels for a talk. That's where Shannon is now."

"Oh, wow," gasped Holly. "I can't wait to see him again."

Holly thought about the phone call all night. Shannon must not be winning at the shows if Mr. Burns still wanted to sell him. If only she had three hundred dollars! Then she remembered something Mr. Burns had said, and she had an idea. Maybe, just maybe . . .

\* \* \* \* \* \*

Sunnyside Kennels was not very far from Holly's house. It was a neat-looking place and she liked Shannon's new handler right away. The plump little woman's name was Mrs. White. She seemed to know her business.

When Mrs. White opened the door to the kennels, all the dogs barked for attention. Holly looked only for Shannon. At first she couldn't see him because he was lying down. He didn't bother to look up and he seemed to have lost a lot of weight.

"Shannon," Holly called softly. "Shannon, it's me."

Immediately the dog looked interested. He got up quickly and his tail began to wag. Then he started to wiggle all over and make his sing-song noises.

"Do you see that?" Mrs. White said to Mr. Burns. "The vets couldn't find anything wrong with your dog. I figured he might just be unhappy.

I'll bet this young lady could get him to eat."

"Okay, I see that he's perked up considerably," Mr. Burns admitted. "But I still don't see what good she can do him."

"Can I take him out of the cage?" Holly asked eagerly. "Shannon hates being cooped up."

"Why not?" Mrs. White smiled.

Holly unfastened the cage door and Shannon bounced out. He barked joyfully. He tried to lick her face. She bent down to hug him and almost missed what was being said.

"Dogs need love as much as food and water," Mrs. White was saying. "This little lady is the key to making your dog a champion, Mr. Burns. He's a fine animal, but you need help if he's going to win for you."

"What?" Holly said suddenly. "What are you talking about? Do you want me to do something?"

"Mrs. White thinks I should hire you to keep the dog company," Mr. Burns said crossly. "I think it's a crazy idea, but I've tried everything else." The big man sighed and went on. "If you'll come here once a day to visit him, I'll give you twenty dollars a week."

"That sounds wonderful," Mrs. Church beamed. "I'm sure Holly would like to do that."

But Holly said, "No, I won't do it."

Her mom gasped in surprise. "But, Holly," she protested. "I thought you'd be delighted. You could see Shannon every day."

"I suppose you want more money," Mr. Burns growled.

Holly shook her head stubbornly. "No," she said again. "You can't hire me to love Shannon. If he does become a champion, you could just take him away again."

"Then what do you want?" Mr. Burns asked suspiciously.

"I want you to give me the dog," Holly said firmly.

"Give you the dog?" Mr. Burns sputtered. "Why you must think I'm nuts. I know a man named Clark who raises puppies for pet shops. He'd be glad to buy any registered dog for . . ."

"Shannon can still make money for you if I own him," Holly interrupted.

Mr. Burns mouth dropped open. "How?" he demanded.

"You could sell his puppies," Holly explained. "That's what you had in mind from the beginning, wasn't it?"

"What a good idea," Mrs. White nodded. "I'm sure the dog would win if Holly took care of him. A show champion's pups are the real money-makers."

Mr. Burns, however, was frowning. "I don't like it," he complained. "How do I know this dog will win? I'd need some proof before I'd just give him away."

"Yes, I see what you mean," Mrs. White agreed. "We need a way for Holly and Shannon to prove themselves to you." The woman thought for a minute. "I have it," she said suddenly. "There will be a dog match over in Orange County in three weeks. We could show the dog there and see if Holly really does make a difference."

"Hmmm," said Mr. Burns. He was still frowning. "I might be convinced if the dog won the entire match."

"Won the match?" Mrs. White objected. "That's asking for quite a bit. This dog is thin and out of condition. What if he just wins his class or Best of Breed?"

"No," said Mr. Burns. "I've wasted enough time and money on this dog. This is his last chance. If he wins this match, I'll give him to Holly on the agreement that I get his pups. If he loses, I'm calling Mr. Clark."

"But we only have three weeks," Mrs. White said desperately.

"That's *your* problem," Mr. Burns sneered. "You've heard my offer. Take it or leave it."

"Since it's Shannon's only chance, we'll take it," Holly said seriously.

# Chapter
# NINE

Mrs. White figured that Shannon would improve faster at Holly's house than in a cage. She sent along special high-protein dog food and coat conditioners. Holly had to agree to bring him back every afternoon so that the woman could help her with him.

Mornings, Holly and Terri took Shannon to the park or the woods. They let him chase the squirrels and the Frisbees. He ate eagerly and he put on weight.

Mrs. White was pleased with his improvement, but she was still worried. "If only we had more time," she said often.

Shannon had to learn to show himself

correctly as well as get into condition. He was a good dog and he always did what Mrs. White told him. Still, there was a problem. His mind was always on where Holly was. He would not trot out proudly unless he was heading toward her.

Finally, Mrs. White said, "I think you are going to have to show him, Holly. Then he won't have to worry about where you are."

"Oh, no," Holly gulped. "I don't know how. I'd mess him up!"

"Not if I teach you how," Mrs. White smiled.

Holly shrugged. "Well, I suppose I could try."

"Good. Then come here and take his leash," the trainer directed. "Now try to make him trot in a straight line."

Holly took the leash and started to walk fast. Shannon walked as close to her as possible.

"No, that won't do," Mrs. White called. "You've got to go faster. The judge wants to see him trot. Come on, faster!"

Holly had to run very fast before Mrs. White

was satisfied. Otherwise, Shannon loafed along and his "gait" dragged.

Mrs. White also pointed out another problem. When Shannon was close to Holly's leg, his body seemed to wrap itself around her. That made his body look crooked. They had to teach him to stay just the right distance from her, and that wasn't easy. But at last Shannon was moving correctly.

Holly learned to "stack" the dog next. Whenever the dogs were still during the show, they had to be posed very carefully. Holly learned to remove the leash, place Shannon's head at just the right level, lift him up under the chest, and place his back feet at right angles to the ground. Finally, she needed to hold his tail so that the long hairs called "feathers" would fall in the most beautiful way.

Each day Holly and Shannon improved. Mrs. White began to sound more confident. "This is just a match," she told them. "You've both worked hard and you have a good chance of winning."

Then it was time for the show. Holly's dad wanted to see Holly show the dog, too. He even offered to pick up Terri. Mrs. White had several other dogs to show, so she would meet them there, later.

"Are you scared?" Terri asked as soon as she got in the car.

Holly managed a weak smile. "No, my face is always green like this," she answered.

"Well, Shannon looks great and that's what matters," Terri said cheerfully.

"You must try to relax," Mrs. Church told Holly. "Mrs. White thinks that you'll win."

"But Mr. Burns doesn't," Holly remembered.

"You'll show him," Terri said confidently.

The show was bigger than Holly had expected. Mrs. White had called it "just a match," but there were five different rings set up for judging. There seemed to be dogs everywhere.

They found Mrs. White and her dogs under a big tree at the edge of the show area. The dogs were in cages except for a sheltie she was

grooming. The woman was carefully back-combing the sheltie and spraying its hair.

"Hi, how's Brandi today?" said Holly, giving the dog a pat on the head.

"Brandi is fine, but I'm a wreck," laughed Mrs. White. "I always am before a show."

"You, too?" Holly's mom said in surprise. "Why, you're a professional."

"That's half the fun," Mrs. White bubbled. "Crazy, isn't it?"

Just then Mr. Burns walked up with a small, sloppy-looking man. He introduced the man as Mr. Clark. Everyone stopped smiling and Shannon's tail stopped wagging.

"Still think you'll win?" the big man said to Holly.

"She has a very good chance," Mrs. White said quickly.

"Then you haven't heard," he went on.

"Heard? Heard what?" Holly's dad demanded.

"Frank Collins is here with that dog called

Elmwood Impressive," Mr. Burns said deliberately.

"What's *he* doing here?" Mrs. White gasped. "That dog has seven points already."

The big man shrugged. "I guess Frank had several younger Scotties that he wanted to bring for experience. He probably brought Impressive along to show off."

Mrs. White looked very worried. "You know we never expected competition like this when Holly made her deal. Surely you can't expect Shannon to beat Frank's dog."

Mr. Burns just laughed. "Oh, but I do. To be a champion, he'll have to beat dogs like Impressive someday. Why not today?"

"But Shannon isn't at his best, yet," Mrs. White protested.

"Tough," the big man sneered. "I called Clark here as soon as I heard about Impressive. He'll be around after the show to pick up this mutt."

"Good luck, little girl," Mr. Clark said coldly.

"If he wins a ribbon here, it might give my kennel class."

As the men walked off, Holly's mom demanded, "What's wrong? Who is this Frank Collins?"

"And what about this dog named Impressive? Are seven points good?" Holly's dad wanted to know.

"Does Holly still have a chance?" Terri worried.

Holly was too afraid to say anything.

Mrs. White hesitated. Then she said, "I hate to tell you about it because Holly is already nervous. Yes, they still have a chance. Shannon is a very nice dog, but . . ."

"But what?" Holly begged.

"But Frank's Scottish terrier is a fantastic dog. Impressive has already won so many titles at important shows that he has seven points. It takes fifteen points to earn the title of 'champion.'"

"Oh, no," Holly groaned. "Now we don't have a chance at winning. And that Mr. Clark is waiting around like a vulture. What's the use?"

"Now just a minute," Mrs. White said sternly. "You don't have to think about beating that Scottie, yet. First you've got to win Shannon's class. Then you have to win Best of Breed and Best of Group. This is no time to give up."

"But it looks so hopeless," Holly said sadly. "How can I beat all those experienced handlers?"

"You don't have to," Mrs. White reminded her. "Have faith in your dog. Shannon is a beautiful animal and you should be proud of him. The judges will do the rest."

Holly nodded. "I suppose you're right. If I don't at least try, I'll lose Shannon for sure."

# Chapter
## TEN

Mr. and Mrs. Church decided to sit in the bleachers and watch Brandi's class. Holly was too nervous to sit so she and Terri took Shannon for a walk. When they got back, Brandi had already won her class and Best of Breed. She was just entering the ring to compete with the other Herding Group winners.

The little brown and white sheltie trotted proudly and posed beautifully. The expression on her face was very sweet. Everyone loved her, and still she lost the competition.

"Poor little Brandi," Holly said as they followed Mrs. White back to the cages.

Mrs. White laughed, "I'm sure Brandi doesn't

care and I still love her. Now it's time to get Shannon ready."

The trainer put Brandi back in her cage and began Shannon's final grooming. She paid special attention to the long hair on his tail and legs. She wiped out his eyes and used a special spray to make his coat shine. At last he was ready.

"This is it," she told Holly. "Put on your number and let's go."

There was a class of golden retriever puppies in Ring 2 when they arrived. The puppies were cute and funny. One wanted to sit down all the time and another wanted to bark. Everyone enjoyed watching them.

Shannon's class was next! There were only four dogs in it, but Holly had to force herself to go in. They were the last ones to check in with the ring steward.

The judge was an elegant young woman. She glanced at the dogs briefly. Her nod sent them trotting around the ring. Shannon wanted to catch up with the dog ahead of him, but Holly managed to hold him back. Then the handlers were to stack the dogs. Holly was glad the judge waited because Shannon was wiggly.

When everyone was ready, the judge walked to the first dog and looked at him from every angle. She felt the dog's mouth, head, ears, shoulders, back, stomach, feet and tail. As the judge got closer to Shannon, he wanted to wiggle even more. He would have turned to sniff the judge if Holly hadn't held him tight.

Now the first dog had to "gait" for the judge. He was to trot away, turn a square corner, and trot along that side. Then it was back to the judge where he was stacked again.

*I've got to get Shannon going fast enough to gait,* Holly said to herself. *But I can't let him get ahead of me on the corners.*

Shannon was getting tired of posing long before the judge was ready for him. When his turn came to trot, he bounded off eagerly. Holly barely caught him before he broke into a gallop.

She knew that was not permissible. Finally, Shannon settled down to an even trot.

When they reached the judge, Holly took forever to pose Shannon. She looked up to see the judge grinning.

"Is this your first time?" the woman asked.

"Uh . . . yes," Holly admitted. *Does it show that much?* she wondered.

"You're doing a fine job," the judge said kindly.

Then the woman made sort of a chirping noise at Shannon. That made his ears raise just a bit and his eyes sparkle. Maybe he thought the judge would throw him a Frisbee. She wrote something on her card and sent Holly back to the end of the line.

Holly stacked Shannon one last time while the judge looked over the class again. At last the woman pointed at Shannon and said, "First . . ."

Holly was so surprised that she didn't hear what else was said. She gave Shannon a big hug. They bounced over to get their pink ribbon.

Her mom and dad were waiting with Terri

and Mrs. White at the edge of the ring. They all tried to hug her at once and made quite a traffic jam for the other dogs.

"Yea, Holly!" Terri squealed, giving her a big hug.

"That's my girl," her dad boomed.

"I'm so proud of you both," her mom told her.

"Nice job!" said Mrs. White.

Holly was half-laughing and half-crying. She was so happy! Then she remembered that this was only the beginning.

"What comes next?" she sniffled.

"After the female golden retrievers are judged, the winners from all the other classes will compete for Best of Breed," Mrs. White answered quickly.

"That sounds scary," Holly worried.

"Not really," Mrs. White assured her. "You just won the class for open males. That makes Shannon the dog to beat."

Holly forced herself to watch the rest of the golden retriever classes. She thought the winner of the "Open Female" class was beautiful. The female's coat was much nicer than Shannon's.

Mrs. White must have guessed what she was thinking because the trainer whispered, "Shannon's head is better. That's important!"

Sure enough, Shannon won the Best in Breed class easily.

"Now things will get harder," warned Mrs. White. "There are always some nice dogs in the Sporting Group at this show."

"Do you suppose Mr. Burns was watching?" Holly asked nervously.

"I'm sure he was. He's coming this way," her mom pointed out.

"Oh, gosh. I don't want to face him or Mr. Clark right now," Holly said weakly. "I'm going to take Shannon off somewhere and just be alone with him."

Mrs. White nodded. "No need to let those men upset you or the dog."

Quickly, Holly and Shannon slipped into the crowd. They found a quiet spot under a tree far away from Ring 2. Holly sat down and Shannon lay with his head in her lap.

"Oh, Shannon, I'm so afraid I'll lose you again," she told him. "What will I do then?"

But Shannon looked happy and licked her face. He didn't seem worried at all.

It seemed only minutes later when Terri came racing up. "You're hard to find," she panted. "They'll be judging the Sporting Group any minute. Come on."

"Oh, gosh," Holly remembered. "I'd better hurry. Mrs. White will at least want to run a towel over Shannon."

Mrs. White met them with her towel and her spray bottle. "There you are," she said nervously. "We have no time to waste. Hold him still while I shine him up a bit."

As she groomed Shannon, Mrs. White continued. "Now listen to me, Holly. I want you to stay as far away from the man with the springer spaniel as possible."

"Why?" Holly asked curiously.

"There's nothing to worry about," Mrs. White

said matter-of-factly, "except that man is known for his bad ring manners. I don't want him upsetting you or Shannon."

Holly nodded and hurried to join the group outside the ring.

# Chapter
# ELEVEN

Eight dogs were waiting to enter the ring for the Best of Group competition. All of their handlers looked friendly except for one. The man with the springer spaniel had thick glasses that covered beady little eyes. The set of his jaw said that he would win any way he could.

Holly hoped the man would go first, but he didn't. Then she hung back still hoping he would go ahead of her.

Finally, he snarled at her, "What are you waiting for, kid? Christmas?"

Holly gulped, "I'm sorry," and hurried into the ring with Shannon. The man with the spaniel was right on her heels. He barely gave her enough room to stack her dog.

The judge was coming now. He gave them both a long look. "Sir," he said to the man with the spaniel, "Please take your dog to the head of the line."

The man looked pleased. *Has he won already?* Holly thought.

But the judge gave Holly a sly wink. He had guessed her problem. Now she had a chance to do her best. She settled down and posed Shannon extra carefully each time. He moved out beautifully when they trotted. The final lineup seemed to take forever. The judge kept pacing back and forth. The crowd waited quietly.

Holly was about to burst from the suspense when the judge pointed at Shannon. The crowd broke into a round of applause. Holly picked up her ribbon in a happy daze.

As Holly stumbled out of the ring with Shannon, her cheering section came alive. "Honey, that was wonderful," said her dad.

Mrs. White sighed with relief. "Thank heaven

your judge saw what was going on. I was awfully worried about you."

"That guy with the spaniel was a real fink," Terri said angrily.

When everyone was quiet again, Mrs. White said earnestly, "The next class is the 'biggie.' It won't be easy. That dog, Impressive, is in top form today. I hope we can do it, but I'm worried."

"We've got to win. We've just got to," Holly moaned.

"I'm sure you can do it," her mom said encouragingly.

"Go get 'em, Shannon," chanted Terri.

"Time to go again," said Mrs. White.

The others could give her pep talks and kind words. Still she and Shannon had to face the test alone. All she could do was her best. She prayed that would be enough.

The dogs outside the ring this time were all special. The Yorkshire terrier was the cutest little mop Holly had ever seen. The Afghan hound was terribly sleek. The dalmation was flashy.

However, the black Scottie known as Impressive was in a class by himself. He had that something extra that says "I'm a star." Next to him, Shannon was just a big lovable dog.

Holly saw that her mom was giving her a "V for victory" sign, but where was her dad? *How strange,* she thought.

Just then the ring steward said, "May we have the winner of the Sporting Group, please?"

*This is it,* Holly thought desperately. *I've got to be the first one in. Yuk.*

Minutes later seven handlers were posing their dogs carefully. It was interesting to see how different their styles were. The Yorkshire's handler had to get down on her knees and pick up her little dog several times. Her comb was never still.

The dogs' gaits were all different, too. The Afghan covered the ring in effortless strides. The Yorkshire's long hair covered his legs so that the little mop just flowed forward. The Scottie seemed to strut.

*What a ham he is!* Holly thought.

Holly was thankful that Shannon did exactly what she asked of him. Most of the time she had him looking his best. Still, as the dogs took their final pose, Holly began to feel sick to her stomach. She could see that the judge loved Impressive. The man had barely glanced at Shannon.

When the judge began to speak, everyone grew quiet. "Ladies and gentlemen," he began. "I have enjoyed this class very much. Never have I seen so many quality dogs outside of a recognized show. I wish I could give them all the prize, but only one can win. Luckily, there is a truly exceptional dog in this class. I am awarding Best of Show honors to the Scottie."

The crowd applauded loudly, but a knife seemed to stab at Holly's heart. She barely managed to walk out of the ring. Shannon caught her mood and seemed to slink at her side.

Her mom handed her a big hanky and hugged Holly. "I'm so sorry. You and Shannon did such a good job," her mom murmured.

Terri was crying, too. Even Mrs. White had tears in her eyes.

"You did your best," the trainer agreed.

Holly couldn't take anymore. She wasn't going to hang around and hand Shannon over to Mr. Clark. She reached down to give the dog a quick hug and put his leash in Mrs. White's hand. Then she ran.

She reached the car and let the waves of misery wash over her. How could she lose Shannon after all they'd been through? Then she heard Terri calling her.

"Holly, Holly, wait until you hear," Terri called breathlessly. But Holly just cried harder. She didn't want to talk to anyone.

"Holly, your dad has something to tell you," Terri panted as she grabbed hold of Holly's shoulders. Just then a big furry mass launched itself at Holly and almost licked her to death.

"Shannon, what are you doing here?" Holly gasped. "Didn't Mr. Clark want you?"

Holly's dad hurried over to her. "Somebody

grab that dog," he panted. "I just paid a lot of money for him."

"What? But you said we couldn't afford him," Holly commented.

Her dad caught his breath and hugged both Holly and her dog. "I know a couple of champs when I see them even if the judge doesn't. You two were great. Honey, you're going to show that dog some more and we'll be the ones to sell his puppies. How about that?"

"Sometimes I really love your father," Holly's mom bubbled as she caught up with them.

"And he's right about Shannon, too," Mrs. White agreed. "When we get him in really top form, that dog might even beat Impressive."

By now Holly was crying, dancing and hugging everyone. She gave Shannon a big kiss right on the forehead. Once again he broke into his singsong noises.

*   *   *   *   *   *

A very tired Holly stared at the show ribbons as her dad drove home. "I think I'll hang these in the garage," she said happily.

"In the garage?" her mom protested.

"Sure. That's where Shannon lives and they're his," Holly explained.

"Oh, no," said her dad firmly and smiling. "Any dog that valuable sleeps in the house."

## About the Author

MARILYN D. ANDERSON grew up on a dairy farm in Minnesota. Her love for animals and her twenty-plus years of training and showing horses are reflected in many of her books.

A former music teacher, Marilyn taught band and choir for seventeen years. She specializes in percussion and violin. She stays busy training young horses, riding in dressage shows, working at a library, giving piano lessons, and, of course, writing books. Marilyn and her husband live in Bedford, Indiana.

Mrs. Anderson's other books include *Come Home, Barkley* and *Nobody Wants Barkley*.